# COCAINE

## BY GERALDINE AND HAROLD WOODS

A GROLIER COMPANY

FRANKLIN WATTS
NEW YORK LONDON TORONTO SYDNEY 1985
A FIRST BOOK

Map: Copyright © 1985 Time Inc. All rights reserved.
Redrawn by Vantage Art, Inc.

Photographs courtesy of: Drug Enforcement Agency (DEA):
pp. 6, 29, 30, 39, 41;
AP/Wide World: pp. 14, 15, 26,
36, 45, 46, 48; Religious News Service:
pp. 19, 52 (Chris Sheridan), 55.

Library of Congress Cataloging in Publication Data

Woods, Geraldine.
Cocaine.

(A First book)
Includes index.
Summary: A study of the effects and abuse of the
drug cocaine, a history of the use of cocaine and its
trade, and a discussion of treatments for cocaine
addiction.
1. Cocaine—United States—Juvenile literature.
2. Cocaine habit—United States—Juvenile literature.
3. Drug abuse—United States—Juvenile literature.
[1. Cocaine. 2. Drug abuse] I. Woods, Harold.
II. Title.
HV5825.W574 1985        362.2'93        85-15523
ISBN 0-531-10035-9

6

# CONTENTS

# INTRODUCTION

No one ever thought Susan would get into trouble. A good student, she starred in many high school plays and sang in dozens of glee club shows. She traveled all around the world with her family, and attended a fine college. On the surface, it seemed as though Susan had it made.

That was before cocaine entered the picture. Susan first tried the drug at age twenty, when a date offered her a small dose. In spite of the fact that cocaine is illegal, Susan accepted. She didn't feel anything special; cocaine affects some people that way the first few times they try it. Unfortunately, a few years later Susan came into contact with the drug again. She was working on a luxury ocean liner in the Caribbean. Her friends on the ship often took coke, and shared the drug with the attractive young woman. Although she was soon taking it daily, Susan convinced herself that there was no problem, since she never actually bought the drug herself.

Gradually, however, Susan's old friends disappeared from her life and were replaced by a fast crowd. Susan later referred to her new group of friends as the "Fast Lane Club."

There were several drug pushers in the "club," and one businessman whom Susan became very involved with. The businessman supplied Susan with as much cocaine as she wanted. Then one day he found a new girl friend, leaving Susan with a broken heart and a heavy cocaine habit.

Susan began to deal drugs herself, to supply the five hundred to fifteen hundred dollars a day she and her friends needed for cocaine. She also began to mix cocaine with heroin, another addictive drug. Susan's health began to suffer; once she stayed "high" for seven days, even though she was suffering from a dangerous disease—hepatitis—at the time. Then she began to vomit blood. A counselor at a drug clinic told her firmly that she would have to give up cocaine or risk death. Susan left the clinic, and took another dose of coke.

Six months later, Susan woke up on the floor of a nightclub. An argument had broken out between several drug dealers. After guns were drawn, Susan's friends knocked her out so that she would not become involved in the fight. As Susan got slowly to her feet, she realized that her handbag had been stolen. She had no money, no keys, and nowhere to go.

Luckily, Susan's mother stepped in to help her daughter. She took Susan to a drug treatment center. Now, four years later, Susan is drug free. She works as a counselor to other addicts who need help kicking their habits.

Steven O'Brien, while working as a police officer in New Jersey several years ago, was chasing a suspect for a minor crime. Suddenly a shot rang out. The shot came from O'Brien's own gun; his own finger was on the trigger.

O'Brien later said that it was fortunate no one was hurt. There had been no real reason to shoot. The suspect was not dangerous, and probably could have been caught peacefully at another time. To all involved, the most horrifying thing about the incident was that O'Brien had fired without even realizing what he was doing. He was completely out of control, because he had taken cocaine before the chase began.

It was not the first time O'Brien had tried coke. At the age of sixteen he had experimented with several types of illegal drugs. At seventeen, he used cocaine for the first time, and took the drug many times during the next two years. However, when it came time to choose a career, Steven O'Brien knew he wanted to join the police force. So he gave up his habit, and remained completely drug free for several years.

Finally, the pull of the drug became too strong for him. O'Brien began to take cocaine every day, and sometimes even several times a day. Soon he needed up to five hundred dollars a week to support his habit—much more than a police officer's salary. So O'Brien, a man sworn to uphold the law, turned to crime. He took bribes, and accepted protection money from drug pushers and other criminals.

Eventually, Officer O'Brien was arrested, tried, and convicted. Cocaine had been even more expensive than he realized. It had cost him his career as a police officer.

These are true stories of two people* who are part of a trend that is sweeping the country—a huge increase in the popularity of cocaine. This trend continues in spite of the fact that cocaine is illegal. Buying, selling, or using the substance is against the law in every state. Penalties range from forced attendance at a drug-treatment program to heavy prison sentences.

*The names used here are not the people's real names.

3

Consider these facts:

☐ Between 1980 and 1982, the number of Americans who have used cocaine jumped from ten to twenty million.

☐ Of all the high school students in the United States, 5.8 percent have tried cocaine at least once.

☐ Experts estimate that five thousand people a day take coke for the first time.

☐ The number of people in treatment for serious cocaine dependency rose from two thousand in 1975 to twelve thousand in 1983.

Although statistics tell only part of the story, they do point up a serious problem we as a nation are now facing—a problem with cocaine.

# 1

## THE DRUG
## AND
## ITS EFFECTS

Cocaine is a white substance that looks like powdered sugar. It has a sharp odor, and is normally sold in tiny plastic bags. *Coca*, the plant from which cocaine is made, is the world's only known natural *local anesthetic.* A local anesthetic numbs the part of the body it touches without putting the patient to sleep. Cocaine, which is stronger than coca, deadens pain wherever it is applied. If cocaine is spread inside the mouth, for example, the mouth will feel "frozen," just as it does when a dentist gives an injection before filling a tooth. Over 150,000 operations a year are performed with cocaine, particularly those involving the eye, ear, nose, and bowels. However, even under controlled medical conditions, cocaine is a very dangerous drug. In 1983, fifteen people died after being given cocaine by their doctors during operations. Because of this, newer, safer local anesthetics, such as *novocaine* and *lidocaine*, are often used in place of cocaine for medical purposes.

### HOW THE DRUG IS TAKEN

Cocaine is usually inhaled, or *snorted.* The user separates the white powder into extremely fine particles, often "cutting" the

*Cocaine, a white powder, is usually sold in small packets.*

drug over and over with a sharp razor blade. After the cocaine is cut, it is usually arranged into thin lines an inch or two in length. With a narrow straw, a tiny spoon, or perhaps a tightly rolled dollar bill, the user inhales the drug into one nostril at a time.

Occasionally, the cocaine is sprinkled on a marijuana or tobacco cigarette and smoked. Since cocaine burns poorly, this method wastes most of the drug's power. A more efficient method of smoking the drug is *freebasing.* The cocaine is boiled with baking soda and other substances; then it is cooled and dried. This process separates the cocaine "base" from other chemicals. The base is then put into a water pipe and heated. An extremely strong concentration of the drug floats above the mixture, and is inhaled from the pipe.

A few people inject cocaine. The drug is mixed with water and placed in a hypodermic needle. The user looks for a blood vessel, usually on the arm or leg, and injects the cocaine directly into the bloodstream.

## THE EFFECTS OF THE DRUG

Besides being a local anesthetic, cocaine is a *stimulant.* It stimulates, or speeds up, the body's nervous system. After taking the drug, the heart beats 30 to 50 percent faster. The breathing rate increases, and the body's temperature rises. Cocaine also narrows blood vessels, so blood pressure rises and blood flow to the arms and legs decreases.

Cocaine also affects the brain. The human brain contains about thirteen billion nerve cells, which are separated from each other by tiny gaps called *synapses.* Chemicals such as *dopamine, norepinephrine,* and *epinephrine* are produced in the brain cells. Though no one understands the process completely, these chemicals seem to transmit "messages" throughout the brain. When a "message" is ready to be sent, the chemicals flow into the synapses between one brain cell and another. After this, the chemicals are drawn back into the brain cells. According to one theory, cocaine may cause these chemicals to remain in the synapses between brain cells longer than usual. This causes the brain's "messages" to be transmitted more rapidly.

Brain chemicals also influence our moods. Happiness, fear, sadness, and other emotions can be affected by changes in the brain chemicals. Cocaine seems to do exactly that. After taking a dose of cocaine, most users report a strong rush of well-being—a "high." Users feel more energetic and extremely alert. They also experience great self-confidence, an "I can do anything" feeling. They may speak rapidly, and jump from subject to subject.

The length and intensity of a cocaine high seem to depend on the method used to take the drug. When cocaine is inhaled, the effects of cocaine can be felt within a minute or two. Freebasers and those who inject the drug may feel differently within seconds. After ten minutes, the first "rush" is over and the drug begins to wear off. When the high wears off, most people feel depressed, worn out, and irritable. This is called a *crash.* The crash seems to be related to the strength of the cocaine high—the better the feeling under the influence of the drug, the worse the crash. In general, freebasing or injecting the drug gives a stronger high (and deeper crash) than inhaling it.

Some cocaine experiences are unpleasant. Instead of feeling high, the user may feel irritable and nervous. Some users become convinced that they are in terrible danger, or that everyone else is an enemy. One man who had taken cocaine frequently for several months believed that he was constantly being watched. He imagined that the walls and ceiling of his apartment were covered with tiny peepholes. When he walked down the street, he was convinced that the people he passed knew that he had taken the drug and were talking about him. Everywhere he went, he thought he heard the word "cocaine" whispered.

Other people hallucinate under the influence of cocaine. The *hallucinations* (seeing, hearing, or smelling something that isn't there) may be very mild; people often report a sparkling or flickering light at the edge of their vision, or a constant feeling that "something just ran past." However, some users report strange visions: an ashtray that changes into a frying pan and then into a chicken or a telephone with hundreds of holes. In these cases, users often know that they are hallucinating. However, most cocaine hallucinations are close enough to reality to be very believable. Coke users may talk to someone who is not there, or wash their hands in imaginary sinks. A person experiencing a hallucination like this is usually unaware that his or her behavior is abnormal.

This belief in a false reality can be very dangerous if the coke user reacts violently to an imagined danger. One man, convinced that invisible children were inside his floor, began to shoot a gun wildly. Later he went into the street to aim at real people. Another coke user strangled his girl friend, whom he mistakenly believed to be attacking him.

Hallucinations and unpleasant feelings are more common after freebasing or injecting the drug, or after frequent use. However, they can occur even if the cocaine is inhaled. Occasionally, a user's very first experience with the drug is bad.

Though many people use cocaine without harming their bodies, even a single dose of the drug has been known to cause physical problems. Some users grind their teeth, shake, or go into a cold sweat. Others experience nausea, muscle pains, and dizziness. More seriously, cocaine can change the rhythm of the heart beat, and even cause the heart to stop functioning. Also, cocaine can cause *seizures*. During a seizure, the person loses consciousness while the body shakes or becomes rigid. The seizure may last for several minutes. A person who suffers a series of these attacks may be left with permanent brain damage. Like hallucinations, these physical symptoms are more common at high doses, or after heavy use of the drug. However, they are always a possibility, regardless of the size of the dose.

## LONG-TERM EFFECTS

If cocaine is used frequently over a long period of time, the lining of the nose becomes damaged. The nose may become constantly congested (stuffed) and runny. In severe cases, the partition between the nostrils may break. An operation is necessary to repair it.

Heavy users of cocaine often suffer sinus headaches. *Sinuses* are hollow places under the cheek and forehead bones. When they become filled with mucous, it is very painful. Also, regular users of cocaine are more likely to catch colds and other respiratory diseases.

People who freebase may have constant sore throats. Their mouths may be irritated and their tongues swollen and painful. Freebasing can also cause permanent damage to the lungs. Those who inject cocaine risk many deadly diseases that can be spread by dirty needles—tetanus, hepatitis, and AIDS (Acquired Immune Deficiency Syndrome).

As mentioned above, heavy users of cocaine, particularly

those who inject or freebase the drug, run great risk of heart problems, seizures, and psychological problems. One particular effect of long-term use is *coke bugs*—the feeling that there are small animals inside the skin. Some users scratch whole layers of skin off, or even burn themselves, trying to get rid of the imaginary creatures. One Hollywood actress had to have plastic surgery after she clawed her face open trying to kill the "bugs." Another coke user scratched deep into his skin, and then used his fingernails and the head of a pin to fish for imaginary germs at the bottom of each wound.

## OVERDOSES

An overdose of cocaine occurs when the body absorbs too much of the drug too quickly. Some doctors compare the condition to a fuse "shorting out" when too much electricity is used in the house. The person who is overdosing loses control of bladder and bowels, and begins to have seizures. Soon, the person passes into coma, a state of deep unconsciousness. If no help is given, the user dies. An overdose reaction can occur within a few minutes or up to an hour after taking the drug. Unfortunately, there is seldom any warning. Some drugs cause mild or moderate reactions before the point of overdose is reached, but not cocaine. Usually, a person overdosing on cocaine passes directly from a feeling of well-being into a seizure.

Some people assume that only freebasers or those who inject cocaine can overdose, but this is not true. Snorting is also dangerous. In one study of twenty-three coke deaths at a particular hospital, researchers found that eleven people had died after injecting the drug, seven after swallowing it, and five after snorting it. Moreover, there is no way to tell exactly what amount of cocaine will cause an overdose. Doctors generally agree that a gram (.035 ounce), taken within a short period of time, will cause death. Yet people have died from much smaller doses. Also, the body's ability to tolerate cocaine can change from day to day. Some users have died from exactly the same doses of cocaine they had taken many times before.

Because so many more people are using cocaine, the number of users who go to hospital emergency rooms for treatment has more than doubled in the last four years. The National Institute for Drug Abuse counted more than six thousand emergency cases in 1983 alone. In the same year, 273 people in Boston, Los Angeles, and Detroit died from the effects of the drug. In the same cities, there were only 109 deaths four years earlier.

Some drug users believe that they can treat a friend's overdose themselves, at home, without a doctor's help. Stories circulate among coke users about supposed remedies: a cold shower, an injection of salt or sugar water, a dose of heroin, sleeping pills or tranquilizers. However, none of these will really help someone who is overdosing on cocaine. The only safe course is to get the victim to a hospital immediately. If the user is having trouble breathing, *mouth-to-mouth resuscitation* or *artificial respiration* (first aid techniques in which air is forced into and out of the victim's lungs) should be used until the doctor can take over.

## OTHER PROBLEMS

Buying drugs from a pusher is very risky. Users have no way of knowing exactly what they have bought. The cocaine used by doctors is extremely pure. Street cocaine, on the other hand, is usually mixed with cheaper substances so the dealer can make more profit. These substances vary from dealer to dealer and from batch to batch. Milk sugar, quinine, and baby laxatives are often added to cocaine; so are other drugs such as *amphetamines*, *lidocaine*, and *procaine*. Besides adding fillers, some dealers simply substitute another drug entirely. Some of the substitute drugs are safe; others are not.

In the same way, the dosage of a street drug is always uncertain. A bag of "cocaine" bought from a pusher may contain from 5 to 40 percent of the drug. So a thin line of white powder from one batch of drugs may have eight times as much cocaine as a line from another batch. The chances of experiencing a bad reaction increase with higher doses, but users have no way of knowing how much cocaine they are really taking.

Cocaine also reacts badly with certain other drugs. People who drink alcoholic beverages while they are under the influence of cocaine increase their chances of having a seizure. This is because alcohol depresses, or slows down, the body's nervous system. In a way, the two drugs give opposite signals to the body. The cocaine speeds up the nervous system while the alcohol slows it, and the body reacts with a seizure. Other drugs that depress the nervous system, like *heroin* and sleeping pills, have the same effect. Yet frequent cocaine users often become very jittery, particularly during the cocaine crash. Many of these people take depressants to ease their nerves—the very drugs they should avoid. Some even take heroin and cocaine at the same time. This mixture is called a *speedball*, and it can be deadly. The comedian John Belushi died from the effects of a speedball. Another danger is that users often become addicted to the heroin or sleeping pills they have taken to combat the cocaine crash.

Opposite: *the casket of actor John Belushi is carried from the West Tisbury Congregational Church on Martha's Vineyard, Massachusetts. Belushi's death in March 1982 was caused by a combination of cocaine and heroin. Above: comedian Richard Pryor almost lost his life in an explosion while freebasing.*

Another famous comedian, Richard Pryor, almost lost his life because of cocaine. Pryor is said to have been heating a freebase mixture when the chemicals exploded, severely burning his body. Freebasing is extremely dangerous because many of the freebase ingredients catch fire easily, especially when they are handled by inexperienced people.

Cocaine is especially dangerous for pregnant women. The drug affects the nervous system of the unborn baby, and may cause the child to be abnormally tense and nervous.

Finally, cocaine and automobiles are a hazardous combination. It is dangerous to drive under the influence of any drug that produces a high, but drivers who have taken cocaine run an especially great risk of having an accident. The problem is that coke users feel so sure of themselves. Yet the drug can cause hallucinations and damage the driver's ability to brake and steer the car. Since few hospitals test for cocaine after fatal accidents, no one knows how many crashes can be blamed on the drug. However, it is believed that the number of cocaine-related accidents is rising every year.

# 2

---

## COCAINE
## ADDICTION

The little monkey was very thin. His ribs could be seen under his fur, which was dull and very tangled. He was starving, and near death. In the monkey's cage were two levers—pieces of metal just the right size to be pushed by a tiny paw. The monkey had been carefully taught how to use both levers. As the scientists watched, the monkey sat for hour after hour, moving one of the levers up and down. The other lever would have brought food into his cage, but the monkey ignored it. The one he concentrated on brought him what he wanted more than food, even more than life: cocaine.

### THE COCAINE HABIT

The researchers who observed the monkey were studying drug addiction. They found that some animals will press a lever more than thirteen thousand times for a single dose of cocaine. Animals will do this until the amount of drug in their bodies is so great that they die from overdose. This does not happen with any other drug. Animals accustomed to receiving heroin, for example, willingly press levers or perform other actions in order to receive a dose. However, they stop before the overdose level is reached.

The research with monkeys showed the incredibly powerful attraction cocaine can have. Though many people are able to take the drug from time to time without becoming dependent on it, others behave just like the monkey in the experiment. They go to incredible lengths to obtain the drug—even to the point of death.

In spite of this, many drug experts still don't consider cocaine an addictive drug. Scientists usually classify a drug as addictive if the habit seems to arise from a physical need. In physical *addiction* the body changes after using certain drugs over and over again. The drug actually becomes part of the body's chemical makeup. It is needed to make the body feel normal. Amphetamines, which stimulate the nervous system the way cocaine does, are a good example of this process. When a person first uses amphetamines, he or she is restless and unable to sleep. After several doses, the user sleeps normally again. In fact, a regular amphetamine user may find it difficult to sleep without the drug. Sleeplessness like this is called a *withdrawal symptom*. Withdrawal symptoms are unpleasant sensations that occur when an accustomed drug is withdrawn. People who are addicted to amphetamines and other drugs take frequent doses partly to avoid withdrawal symptoms.

Another sign of the body's adaptation to a drug is *tolerance*. Since the body has made the drug part of its regular chemistry, the usual dose no longer produces the drug's special effect. For example, if a person regularly takes heroin, the nerve cells change. They become more excitable, perhaps in preparation for the calming drug to come. The person feels

more and more nervous, and larger and larger doses of heroin are needed to create a peaceful feeling.

Regular users of cocaine do feel mild withdrawal symptoms when they go without the drug. Tiredness, hunger, chills, and nausea are common. However, the withdrawal itself does not appear to be the reason cocaine users take the drug again. Also, users do not build up tolerance to cocaine. Some people do take larger and more frequent doses of the drug, but not because their normal dose has lost its power. Instead, they seem to be seeking more intense thrills from the drug.

Many scientists believe that the need for cocaine seems to be much more mental than physical. This type of drug habit is usually called psychological *dependency*. Psychological dependency is no less powerful or dangerous than physical addiction. In many ways, it is stronger. People who are psychologically dependent on cocaine can think of little else. Their whole lives become focused on the drug. They strongly crave the good feelings a cocaine high can create, and dread the depression of a cocaine crash. Both of these feelings make cocaine habits extremely hard to break.

Recently, a great deal of research has been done about the role our bodies and minds play in the formation of drug habits. Some scientists have come to the conclusion that psychological and physical drug habits are so closely related that they cannot really be placed in separate categories. These researchers call all drug habits "addictions" if they have three characteristics: First, there is an overwhelming need for the drug. Second, the user has no control over the drug. Third, the user continues to take the drug in spite of the problems it causes. By this definition, cocaine is certainly an addictive drug.

# WHO BECOMES DEPENDENT
## ON COCAINE?

In May 1983, Dr. Mark Gold set up a special hotline phone for people who were having problems with cocaine. If someone in any part of the country dialed 800-COCAINE (a toll-free call), the phone would ring in Fair Oaks Hospital in Summit, New Jersey. Dr. Gold wasn't sure if anyone would call, but he arranged to have a counselor near the phone twenty-four hours a day, just in case. The phone did ring—over a thousand times a day, almost four hundred thousand times the first year. No one had guessed that America's cocaine problem was so widespread.

Most users try cocaine once or twice and then stop. Typical of this group is a middle-aged dentist who said that the fast heart beat he felt after sniffing the drug was very frightening. It reminded him too strongly of a heart attack he had had a few years earlier. For this man, one dose of cocaine was enough. Another couple used cocaine four or five times, when it was offered to them at parties. After reading more and more magazine articles about cocaine's dangers, the couple realized that the drug they had considered as harmless as a cocktail was not safe at all. Though they had enjoyed their experiences with the drug, the couple had no trouble saying no when it was next offered to them.

Four or five million Americans continue to take the drug once every month or so, often at a party or other special occasion. No one knows exactly how many users go on to become hooked on cocaine. Estimates range from 10 to 30 percent. That means that between two and six million Americans abuse cocaine.

One of these is a twenty-nine year old investment banker who experimented with cocaine during his college years. Because the drug was so expensive, at first he took it only on special occasions. After beginning his career, however, he used part of each salary to buy the drug. Then, during a period of great pressure at work, the banker's cocaine habit went totally out of control. Soon he needed two thousand dollars a week to support his habit. His health and his marriage suffered. Luckily, his wife finally persuaded him to enter a drug treatment center.

## WHAT CAUSES COCAINE DEPENDENCY?

Why do some people have a "take it or leave it" attitude towards cocaine, while others seek the drug desperately? Researchers all over the world are looking for the answer to that question, with little success. At present, there is no reliable way to predict which cocaine users will control their doses of the drug, and which will end up being controlled by cocaine. This is because no one yet understands exactly why people become drug addicts.

There are many theories. A cocaine habit may actually be a disease. The idea is that people who are addicted to cocaine, or to any other drug for that matter, seek the drug to make up for some natural substance that is missing in their own bodies. Scientists studying *narcotics* addiction, for example, have found that the brain produces natural painkillers called *endorphins*. The theory is that addicts may not produce enough endorphins of their own. They may take the pain-relieving narcotics as a substitute for the natural endorphins. "Coke-heads'' may use the drug in a similar way, though no one yet can even guess what brain chemicals cocaine might replace.

If addiction is a disease, the tendency to develop it might be inherited. A weakness for a particular drug might be passed from parent to child, just as brown eyes and dark hair are handed down. One study found that children of alcoholics are four times more likely to become alcoholics themselves. This does not mean that everyone whose parent drinks too much will become an alcoholic, or that everyone whose relative has a cocaine habit will become a *cocaholic*. However, people with a family cocaine problem might run a greater risk of abusing the drug.

Another theory is that cocaine abuse is at least partially caused by problems in the addict's personal life. People who have a poor opinion of themselves, who have difficulty making friends, or who handle stress poorly may turn to cocaine as a solution to their problems. The drug may give the user extra confidence and a feeling of being in control of life. Of course, no one's problems will just go away, and neglected problems tend to pile up. More important, the drug user does not get the chance to learn problem-solving skills. So when the drug wears off, users are faced with an even worse situation than before. Many turn to the drug again for more relief; gradually they become unable to cope without it.

Pressures from society may also contribute to this pattern. A thousand times a day, all sorts of drugs are advertised on television. Tired? Try this pill to pep you up. Nervous? This syrup will help you sleep. Does your back hurt, your nose run? Do your eyes itch? The message is always the same: Don't suffer. There is something that will make you feel better immediately. However, there simply aren't any magic ways to change a hard test into an easy one, or to make anyone's family perfect. Even the happiest person will experience some tense or sad times. Yet advertisements tell us that pain is something that should always go away instantly. It's not surprising that some people turn to drugs to make their hard times disappear.

Cocaine also supplies some feelings our society values. In America, self-confident, ambitious people are often admired. Many people accept the "American Dream" of success, wealth, and happiness achieved by hard work. Cocaine often makes people feel energetic and able to do anything. Under the influence of the drug, the "American Dream" appears easier to fulfill. Because of this, cocaine often appeals to people who dislike other drugs—people who want to "make it" instead of dropping out of society.

## OTHER PROBLEMS OF
## COCAINE ADDICTION

It really doesn't matter to someone who is hooked on cocaine whether the habit is caused by mental, physical, or environmental pressures. In fact, just like the monkey, all the cocaholic really cares about is the little bag of white powder. The drug becomes more important than work, personal relationships, and health.

Typically, someone who has a heavy cocaine habit is absent from work often. Since it is difficult to sleep while under the influence of the drug, a user may be overtired after a whole night's session. Regular use of cocaine also decreases appetite, and the effects of the drug may mask other illnesses. So cocaholics tend to lose weight and become run down, leading to poor performance on the job. In one survey of frequent cocaine users, 86 percent reported that they had missed time at work because of the drug, while 37 percent said they had actually lost their jobs because of coke.

One of these is John Drew, who was a forward for the Utah Jazz basketball team. Drew, who admitted taking cocaine, was ordered into a drug treatment program by the team management. He understood that he would be tested for drug use regularly and without warning, and that his career in professional sports was on the line. Nevertheless, he continued to use coke. In December 1984, Drew was dropped from the Jazz after a random drug test showed the presence of cocaine in his urine.

Cocaine has an even more serious effect on relationships with friends and family. Users often find that as their involvement with the drug grows, they begin to spend time only with other people who are interested in cocaine. Friendships with "straight," non-drug users fall apart. Also, couples who depend on cocaine to have a good time together often find that the drug replaces relaxed conversation and real sharing— things that people in love need. Although cocaine has a reputation as an aid to sex, heavy users report that eventually the drug decreases their desire and takes the place of sex entirely. In one survey, 93 percent of people who used cocaine heavily said that the drug had harmed their relationships with others, and 77 percent blamed cocaine for their divorce or separation.

Although the price has dropped considerably, cocaine is still quite expensive—five times the price of gold! Someone with a heavy cocaine habit can easily spend eight hundred dollars a week or more on the drug. Not many people have that kind of money for drugs, and some users turn to crime to support their cocaine use. In one survey conducted by a cocaine

*Kansas City Royals' Willie Wilson served
nearly three months in prison on a
cocaine-related charge. He later said,
"Don't do drugs. Kids can learn from my mistakes."*

hotline, one-half of the callers said they had stolen to pay for the drug. Among heavy users, 52 percent sell cocaine themselves, in order to finance their habit. Other users lose their savings and their property because of the high price of cocaine. Typical of these is the owner of a trucking company who "snorted away" a house and a half-million-dollar bank account before he kicked the habit.

When you consider the price of cocaine and the terrible effects it has had on so many people, its simple origins might surprise you—it comes from a plant that grows wild in the mountains of South America.

# 3

## THE HISTORY
## OF COCAINE

The Andes Mountains cut through South America like a rough spine. Life is hard there: the air on the high slopes is cold and thin, and few crops survive in the mountain soil. However, a plant called *Erythroxylon coca* and a relative, *Erythroxylon novogranatense*, grow wild throughout the area. These bushes, which are commonly called *coca*, reach a height of 12 to 18 feet (3.6 to 5.5 m). Their greenish-brown leaves are oval-shaped. The average coca plant lives for fifty years—longer than many human inhabitants of the Andes.

When they are chewed, the leaves of the coca plants decrease appetite, raise body temperature, and give the user more energy and self-confidence. The people of the Andes use coca to help themselves face the bitter cold and lack of food common in their area. They also chew the leaves to make themselves work longer with less time for rest.

According to archaeologists, this practice began over a thousand years ago. Bundles of mummified coca leaves in carrying pouches have been found; so have ceramic pots in which the leaves were stored. No one knows how the custom of chewing coca leaves began. The ancient Inca Indians of the

*The source for cocaine, the coca plant,*
*grows wild in the Andes mountains.*

area had many legends about the origin of the plant itself. In one tale, a beautiful but disloyal woman was killed, cut in half, and buried. The coca bush sprang up from her remains. In another story the leaves were a gift from the sun god Inti, who asked his moon mother Moma Quilla to plant coca bushes on earth.

The Incas valued coca so much that at the height of their empire, coca was considered a special privilege. Only nobles, priests, soldiers going into battle, and those who had been especially courageous were allowed to use the plants. After the Inca Empire fell, coca was again available to anyone who wanted it. The drug was used so widely that it even gave its name to a measure of length. A *cocada* was the distance that could be traveled during the chewing of one bunch of leaves!

## COCA BECOMES COCAINE

In the fifteenth century, European explorers brought descriptions of the coca plant home with them. However, the leaves themselves were seldom imported since they lost their power during the long ocean voyage. As it was difficult to grow coca in the European climate, people who had not visited the New World were unable to experience the effects of the plant.

In the late 1850s, several scientists tried to extract the active ingredient from coca leaves. No one knows who was

*The coca plant can be stripped of its leaves periodically and still live—for an average of fifty years.*

31

the first to succeed. Many believe the credit for turning coca into cocaine belongs to Albert Nieman, a Viennese scientist, who produced the white powder around 1859. The new drug was more concentrated and had a much more powerful effect than the natural coca leaves. In 1859, another European, Paolo Mantegazza, published "The Coca Leaf and Cocaine Papers." Mantegazza reported "flying through colorful visions" under the influence of the drug. He also claimed to have visited 77,438 new worlds "on the wings" of coca.

About twenty years later cocaine was imported to the United States for the first time. European and American doctors began to experiment with the new drug. At that time drug testing was not as advanced as it is today. Few laboratory animals were used; many scientists investigating the effect of a particular drug simply took it themselves or gave some to their assistants. This could be very dangerous. One researcher, William Halstead, noted that three of his employees became addicted to cocaine and died without being able to break the habit. There was also little protection for the consumer during this period, since the government did not test and regulate drugs as it does today. Anyone could buy and use any drug without a prescription. There was no guarantee at all that a new drug was safe or effective.

In 1884, Sigmund Freud, the famous pioneer in the treatment of mental illness, bought .035 ounce (1 g) of cocaine. Freud tried .00175 ounce (.05 g) himself, and gave doses to a few other doctors. A few months later Freud published a report, "On Coca," in which he praised cocaine. Cocaine was also used in the 1890s by another famous (but unreal) person. The fictional detective Sherlock Holmes took the drug in the story "The Sign of the Four."

In the late nineteenth century, doctors prescribed cocaine

for asthma, tiredness, nausea, and many other ailments. Cocaine was also widely used as a treatment for several types of drug addiction. During the American Civil War, in the 1860s, many soldiers were given frequent doses of *narcotics*, drugs that relieve pain, for their wounds. After the war ended, in 1865, so many soldiers remained addicted to those drugs that narcotic addiction became known as "the army disease." Cocaine was given to these addicts, and also to alcoholics, as a cure for addiction. One writer called the drug "the staff" upon which the suffering addict could lean. Unfortunately, while the treatment did relieve some of the painful symptoms addicts experienced without their drugs, it did nothing to lessen the addiction, but only created a new one.

Also in the 1880s, several companies introduced drinks and other products containing cocaine. The Parke-Davis drug company sold a cocaine cigar which was said to give relief from "the blues." Cocaine lozenges, tea, and candies were marketed. Another popular product was Vin Mariani, a mixture of cocaine and wine. Vin Mariani was advertised as "Unequaled . . . for fatigued [tired] or overworked Body and Brain." It was also said to prevent "Malaria, Influenza and Wasting Diseases." Such famous people as President Ulysses S. Grant, inventor Thomas Edison, and Pope Leo XIII drank Vin Mariani.

Though Vin Mariani sold well, some people objected to the fact that it contained alcohol. For them, a soft drink made from soda water, kola nuts, and cocaine was invented. The new beverage, Coca Cola, is still on the market today! However, when the dangers of cocaine became apparent, the company changed the formula. Today's Coke contains no cocaine. *Caffeine*, a drug that excites the body's nervous system and is found in coffee and tea, is added instead.

# REGULATION

By the end of the 1880s, the new wonder drug was beginning to look less than wonderful. Many of the alcoholics and narcotic addicts who had been treated with cocaine picked up another problem—a cocaine habit. Sigmund Freud wrote other papers on the drug, including "Craving For and Fear of Cocaine," which reported some serious side effects.

One of these was hallucinations. Freud mentioned that frequent users of the drug often felt as if they had "small animals moving in the skin." Some cocaine users also acted strangely; the confidence the drug gave made them feel they could jump over buildings, or perform other impossible acts. Frequent users also became very moody. They were on top of the world one moment and in despair the next. These artificial changes in personality were frightening because they seemed uncontrollable.

Along with these real medical and psychological problems came some fantastic legends about the drug. Some police officers claimed that cocaine users were likely to injure people or damage property while under the influence of the drug. One writer stated flatly that people who took cocaine immediately became criminals. In some areas of the country, rumors spread that cocaine increased criminals' power until they became almost superhuman. A few police departments actually switched to larger bullets in order to prepare themselves for cocaine users who went wild.

More and more magazine and newspaper stories about the danger of cocaine began to appear. A 1911 article in *Hampton's Magazine* was typical. It described a twenty-two-year-old man who had innocently taken a cold medicine containing cocaine. He enjoyed the feeling of well-being the medicine provided, and continued using the drug long after his cold was cured. Soon he was a cocaine addict; his mental and physical health suffered and within a year he was sent to a hospital for the insane.

As its dangers became obvious, the American public demanded that cocaine be outlawed. (The very first law prohibiting coca had been passed by Philip II of Spain in 1573. It was quickly repealed when the Spanish conquerors realized that the South American Indians would trade the little green leaves for gold and silver. During the next three hundred years, there were very few laws regulating coca or cocaine, and none in the United States.) In 1906, the federal government passed the Pure Food and Drug Act. The act required the labels of all medicines to clearly state the alcohol, narcotic, or cocaine content. In 1908, an amendment to the act prohibited shipping those three drugs across state lines. The Harrison Narcotics Act, which was passed in 1914, required anyone who imported, manufactured, or sold narcotics and cocaine to register with the government and pay a special tax. After 1922, no more cocaine could be imported into the United States, and only coca intended for certain medical purposes.

All these regulations cut the use of cocaine tremendously. The medical use of cocaine dropped as newer, safer drugs were discovered. The illegal recreational use of the drug also decreased. For almost fifty years, cocaine was rarely seen "on the street."

## NEW POPULARITY

In the 1960s, the use of many types of illegal drugs increased greatly. A slogan of the day was "turn on, tune in, and drop out." To "turn on" meant to get high on marijuana, LSD,

*Woodstock, the music festival that took place at Bethel, New York, in 1969, was symbolic of the "turn on, tune in, and drop out" movement of the 1960s.*

cocaine, and other drugs. To "tune in" was to expand one's view of the world, to accept all sorts of new ideas. If that happened, one was supposed to "drop out" of mainstream society.

Because cocaine was so much more expensive than other street drugs, it remained rare during much of this period. Many people called cocaine the champagne of the drug world, considering it a luxury reserved for the rich or for special occasions. However, drug traffickers in South America, seeing the drug explosion in the North, began to plant more and more coca bushes. As the supply increased, the price fell, and cocaine use increased.

Alarmed by the huge amounts of illegal drugs in the country, the federal government passed the Controlled Substances Act in 1970. This law divides all drugs into five categories, according to their dangers. Cocaine is a type two drug: of some medical value but likely to cause problems among users.

Throughout the 1970s, most states passed strict laws prohibiting the recreational use of cocaine and providing large fines or long prison terms for people who broke the law. Nevertheless, use of the drug continued to grow, and by the early 1980s, cocaine had become one of the most popular drugs in America.

# 4

## THE
## COCAINE
## TRADE

On November 27, 1984, Dale Lent was walking on an airstrip in the Arizona desert when he saw some fresh tire tracks from a small plane. This seemed odd to Mr. Lent, an off-duty detective, since the airstrip had been abandoned after World War II. He notified the local police, who immediately set up a roadblock. The result: the authorities seized one billion dollars worth of Peruvian cocaine and arrested four smugglers.

### FROM THE FIELD
### TO THE STREET

Dale Lent's quick thinking interrupted a criminal operation that began a continent away. Most of the world's coca is grown in the mountainous regions of Peru, Bolivia, and Columbia. The bottom rung on the smuggling ladder is the grower—usually a poor South American farmer. Bacilia Flores, for example, comes from the mountains of Bolivia. Her husband used to dig potatoes for a living; their income was so small that there was barely enough food for the family. The couple's three children often went naked, because there was no money for clothing.

*A farmer harvesting his coca crop*

In desperation, the couple moved to Chapare, where one-third of the world's coca grows. There, Mrs. Flores cultivates a small plot of coca bushes. Every three months she harvests and dries fifty pounds of coca leaves. She makes ten times more from her crop than her husband used to earn from potatoes. The Flores family hopes to save enough money from their crop to move back to their mountain village and buy a house.

The Flores family, and thousands of other country people, sell their crops to a representative of a smuggling group—a *mule*. The mule has to carry the coca to laboratories where it will be turned into cocaine. The mule first converts the leaves to coca paste. This is done by adding kerosene to the leaves and waiting until the plants dissolve. The coca paste is more concentrated than the plant material, so it is easier to carry. However, it does have disadvantages. Coca leaves are legal in South America, but the paste and other coca products are not. So the mule risks arrest during the journey to the laboratory.

The mule wraps the paste in llama skins or places it in other containers. Sometimes the drug is transported by car; other mules fly small planes to hidden airstrips. The planes dump packages of money on the runways and pick up bundles of coca paste in exchange.

Although coca is grown in several countries, most of the laboratories are located in Colombia. In the labs, chemists add several substances to the coca paste and cook it for a few hours. The mixture becomes more concentrated; at this point it is called coca base. The coca base is washed, strained, and

*Inside a cocaine laboratory*

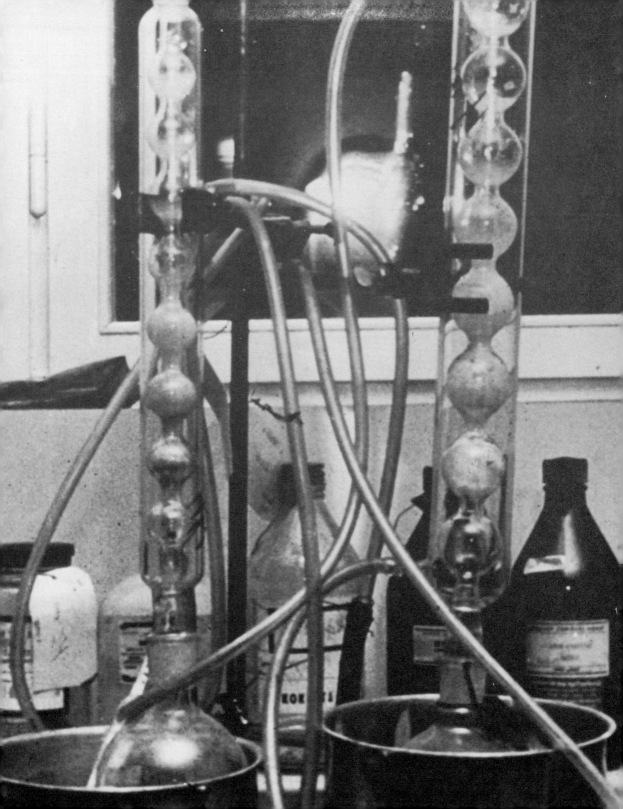

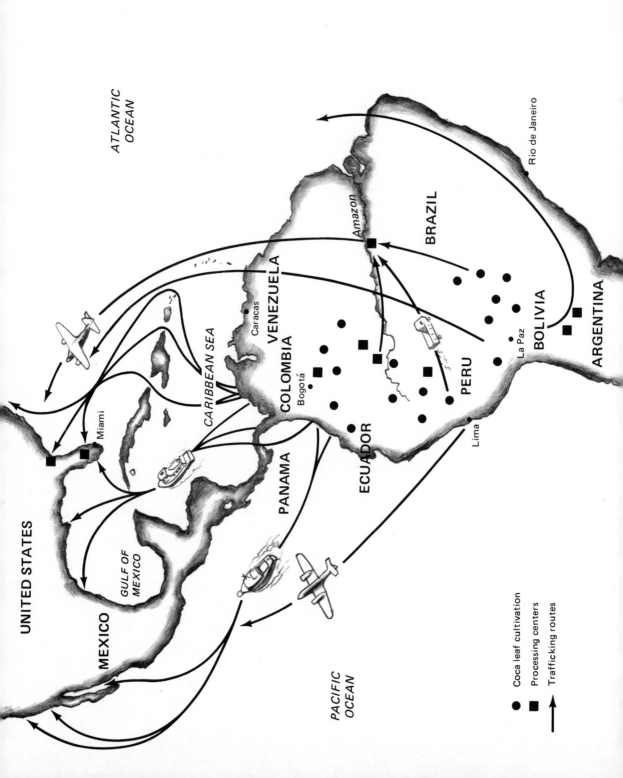

ATLANTIC OCEAN

Rio de Janeiro

BRAZIL

Amazon

VENEZUELA

Caracas

COLOMBIA

BOLIVIA

La Paz

Bogotá

PERU

ARGENTINA

CARIBBEAN SEA

Miami

ECUADOR

PANAMA

Lima

UNITED STATES

GULF OF MEXICO

MEXICO

PACIFIC OCEAN

● Coca leaf cultivation

■ Processing centers

→ Trafficking routes

treated with hydrochloric acid and acetone, the chemical in nail polish remover. The mixture is whitened with bleach and dried in an oven. The cocaine is now ready for sale.

Some cocaine is sold in South America, but most of it is exported to the United States. A portion of the drug is carried across our borders by employees of the smuggling rings. They hide the white powder in hollowed-out shoe heels, inside picture frames, and in rolling pins, or they tape it to their bodies. The smugglers pose as innocent travelers, perhaps vacationers or business people, and try to blend in with the crowd at United States customs checks. The smugglers often carry several sets of false passports, drivers' licenses, and other identification cards.

Large amounts of the drug are also ferried to Florida, Texas, or other southern states in small boats. Other shipments, like the one Dale Lent discovered, are brought by small planes flying low to avoid radar. The boats and planes arrive in unsettled areas away from customs officials entirely, or mix with the crowd in busy marinas or airports.

Once in the United States, the drug is brought to *safe houses*—houses or apartments rented by the smugglers as warehouses for their merchandise. Each safe house has a "sitter" in it. The sitter does nothing but babysit for the cocaine, never leaving the house unless another sitter is present. No customer ever comes near the safe house. Other members of the gang take the drug from the safe house and deliver it to dealers, who in turn sell it to their customers.

Each step of this process increases the value of the drug enormously. Mrs. Flores receives less than ten dollars for every 2.2 pounds (1 kg) of leaves she harvests. The paste the mule carries is worth about $180 a pound ($400 a kg), while the lab's coca base sells for over $4,500 a pound (about

$10,000 a kg). Smugglers who take the product to the United States might charge $9,000 a pound ($20,000 a kg). Once on the street, the cocaine may sell for up to $140,000 a pound ($300,000 a kg).

## ENFORCEMENT PROBLEMS:
## AT THE SOURCE

As cocaine use grows in the United States, the government has designed more and more programs to fight the drug trade. In South America, United States officials have offered aid to the governments of coca-growing countries. Some of the aid is in the form of money, equipment, and advisers to the country's own anti-drug agents. The United States also gives money for roads, schools, and industry in coca regions, hoping that people with a better standard of living will have less need for the income from the drug trade. In the same way, United States experts show farmers other crops they can grow instead of coca.

So far, these anti-drug programs have not been very successful. In the Huallaga Valley of Peru, for example, United States and Peruvian officials cracked down on the drug trade in 1984. The area immediately went into an economic depression. Hundreds of farmers lost their incomes, as did other Peruvians employed by the drug traffickers. Few people wanted to substitute coffee and other crops for coca. The coca plant is basically a weed that will grow anywhere with very little help. Other crops require much more work, and bring in less money. Also, many farmers see no need to change. In their view, drugs are an American problem, best solved in the United States.

After a few months, a revolutionary group called Shining

Colombian police raided this cocaine laboratory
in the jungles of eastern Colombia
in May 1984. Later, they found three tons
of cocaine under the building.

Path began to organize a revolt in Huallaga. The government of Peru, worried about its own survival, withdrew its anti-drug troops and sent in the army to fight Shining Path. The drug trade immediately came back in full force.

Although the government of Peru did its best, not all South American countries are really interested in wiping out the drug trade. In Bolivia, for example, coca brings more money into the country than any other product. Without the drug trade the economy of the country might collapse completely. Also, many officials, from the lowest to the highest level of government, are paid by drug traffickers. In a country where the average police officer earns $25 a month, it is hard to resist drug money. It is also difficult for the United States to work out agreements with some South American governments because they are very unstable. Bolivia alone has had eleven governments in the past seven years. Since 1981, the United States has signed anti-drug treaties with Bolivia, Colombia, Peru, and the Central American country Belize. During the same time period, production of coca rose 40 percent.

## ENFORCEMENT PROBLEMS:
## THE SMUGGLERS

Efforts to control smugglers are not much more successful. The United States Customs Agency has about forty-five

*Nearly two tons of Colombian cocaine worth about $175 million was seized from a warehouse at the Miami International Airport by drug enforcement agents in March 1982.*

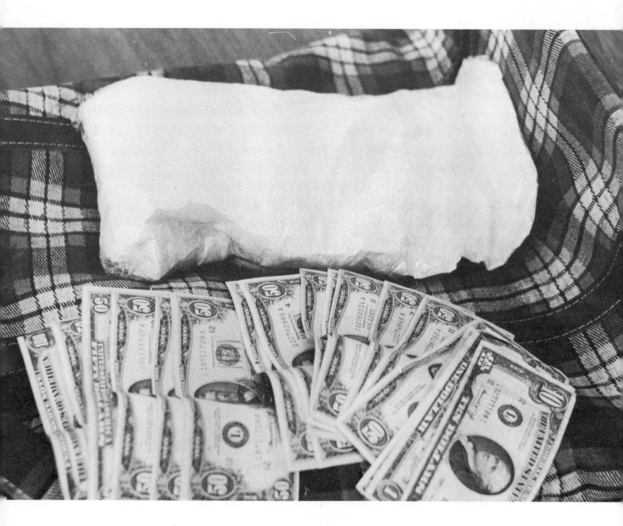

*This money and bag of cocaine were
confiscated from a fifteen-year-old
youth from Chile after his arrival at
Los Angeles International Airport.*

hundred inspectors at airports, docks, train stations, and other points of entry into the country. These forty-five hundred people are in charge of checking 300 million travelers each year. Obviously, not every person who enters the United States can be carefully searched. Instead, the customs agents try to check someone who fits the description of a "typical" smuggler. Yet even this is hard. Many criminals slip by while innocent people are searched.

Agents combating smugglers' boats and planes are also understaffed. The Coast Guard tries to intercept boats carrying illegal drugs into the country. However, it has less than twenty boats patrolling the entire southeast and gulf coasts. Customs also has only twelve planes fast enough to catch smugglers' planes. Eight of these are in Florida, leaving only four to patrol the rest of the American continent. In addition, most drug traffickers' planes fly too low to be detected by conventional radar. Special radar balloons are needed, but there are only three of these along the United States' southern border. Drug enforcement officials estimate that less than 10 percent of the illegal drugs brought into the country is seized.

One of the most effective ways of tracking drug smugglers has been through the banks. In the United States, anyone depositing over ten thousand dollars at one time must be reported to the government. For drug dealers, ten thousand dollars may be less than one day's profit. To avoid detection, many drug dealers use foreign banks, or set up a number of dummy businesses. Moving money through these routes is called *laundering.* After funds have been laundered, they are "clean" and can't be traced. Though many criminals escape, some are caught when their attempts to launder money fail.

# 5

## TREATMENT
## OF COCAINE
## ADDICTION

One day in 1983, twenty-five thousand employees from all the major Hollywood film studios received an unusual paycheck. Tucked into each envelope was an "Awareness card." The card asked if the employee was having problems with cocaine, alcohol, or other drugs. It also urged the employee to seek help if the answer was yes.

The television and movie industry is not the only one concerned about the effects of cocaine and other drugs on its workers. In recent years most of the airlines, the National Basketball Association, many major league baseball teams, and more than five thousand corporations have started drug prevention and treatment programs. Schools, church groups, and other organizations have done the same.

All these programs exist for two reasons. First of all, addiction to cocaine and other drugs is growing. Secondly, those addictions can be successfully treated.

## RESIDENTIAL PROGRAMS

The ranch house on Buttermilk Mountain in Colorado doesn't look like a hospital, but it is: the Aspen Addiction Rehabilitation

Unit of Presbyterian/St. Luke Medical Center. Ten people arrive there each month with assorted suitcases and one heavy burden—a cocaine habit. At the Aspen Center, the patients take some unusual medicine for their condition. They go rock climbing and cross country skiing, balance on logs, and cross streams on ropes. According to the Aspen doctors, the physical activities are designed to teach the patients that they can ask for and receive help from other people. This is important because when the program is ended, the former addicts will still crave the drug from time to time. They will need support from friends, relatives, and counselors to stay away from cocaine.

Buttermilk Mountain is a *residential* or "live-in" treatment program for drug abuse. It is often called a *therapeutic* or heal-ing community—TC for short. There are many therapeutic communities throughout the country. Some treat only people with cocaine habits; others accept people who are addicted to any kind of drug, and people who are having problems with more than one drug. (In street terms, people who take several types of drugs are called *garbage heads*.) Some therapeutic communities, like Buttermilk, are located in beautiful wilder-ness areas. Others, like New York's Phoenix House, are found in crowded cities. Patients who join TCs usually have extreme-ly strong cocaine habits, and need twenty-four-hour-a-day help to overcome their addictions.

When they move into a therapeutic community, drug users change every part of their lives. They leave behind, at least for a while, friends, family, homes, and jobs. This break with normal life is made for a very good reason. While forming drug habits, the patients learned to link the drug with certain people, places, or activities. For example, some users snorted cocaine every evening after work. Others took the drug every time they went to a party with certain friends. For these

people, just the trip home from the office or a telephone call from an addicted friend is enough to set off an intense craving for the drug. By changing the patients' environment, the TC eliminates these reminders of the drug. In a way, the TC fights the "habit" in every drug habit.

Therapeutic communities also provide a strong structure for people whose lives are falling apart. In a typical TC, every moment of the day is scheduled, from wake-up call in the morning to lights-out at night. Patients must follow the timetable strictly; there is no opportunity to go off alone and face the temptation to use the drug again.

The TC schedule may include time for physical activity, such as the rock-climbing at Buttermilk. It may include classes for those who have not yet finished school. (One TC, Phoenix House in New York, operates a live-in high school for teenage drug abusers.) Almost certainly, the schedule will allow time for work—usually a few hours of household chores. The idea is that the patients need to become part of a community where everyone has both rights and duties. By washing dishes, mopping floors, and cleaning bathrooms, the patients are fulfilling their responsibilities to the group.

Responsibility in a TC is encouraged with a system of rewards and punishments. New patients usually begin at the bottom of the TC "ladder," doing unpleasant jobs that no one else wants. After a period of good behavior, patients move up to easier chores. They also receive extra privileges, such as

*Two young people in the rural setting of Pius XII-Holy Cross Campus, a drug rehabilitation center in Rhinecliff, New York*

more television time or a chance to go on trips. TC members who disobey the rules by failing to do their assigned work, breaking the schedule, or lapsing into drug use move down the ladder again. They are reassigned to their old chores, and their privileges are taken away.

An important part of each day in a therapeutic community is counseling. Patients usually meet for an hour or more with a therapist, a doctor or a psychologist who has been trained to help drug abusers understand and change their behavior. Patients are also assigned to small groups where everyone discusses his or her problems. Though each group is led by a therapist, much of the counseling comes from the patients themselves, who support and sometimes challenge each other. Because everyone has a problem with cocaine, the patients can understand exactly what each member of the group is going through. They can also spot excuses or lies easily because chances are they have tried some themselves.

In the same way, therapists at therapeutic communities usually understand drug abusers very well, since most are ex-addicts. They know all the problems and pitfalls cocaholics face during the course of treatment, since at one time they themselves were in the same position. The therapists are also a symbol of hope for recovering addicts; they are living proof that a cocaine habit can be broken.

Treatment time in a residential therapeutic community ranges from as little as twenty-eight days to as long as a year. After leaving the community, the former addicts are often given phone numbers of one or two "buddies" who may be called at any time, day or night, whenever the craving for cocaine appears. Most former addicts also attend therapy sessions once or twice a week, or even more frequently, until

*A group therapy session for drug addicts
at Daytop Village in New York City*

they feel capable of handling the urge to use drugs again. Occasionally, groups of ex-cocaine abusers live together in "half-way" houses. Members attend school or hold jobs, and follow less rigid schedules. However, they have support and help from each other and from visiting therapists.

All this support is needed because cravings for cocaine can last for years. One former cocaholic was giving a lecture on drug abuse when someone placed a bottle of the drug on the table. Although she had been off the drug for four years, the sight of the white powder touched off a strong desire for cocaine. She felt unable to resist temptation while in the same room with the drug, and left the lecture. Another former addict was horrified when someone placed a gift of cocaine on his desk. He did not want to use it, but his craving was so strong that he was actually afraid to touch the drug. He called a friend who came and flushed the cocaine down the toilet.

Though the power of a drug habit is great, it can be broken. Studies show that as many as 75 percent of the patients who complete the treatment program in the best therapeutic communities stay off drugs permanently. However, many patients drop out of the programs too soon and return to drugs.

## OUTPATIENT TREATMENT

It's a storefront, a church basement, a hospital waiting room, or a school gym. It's open twenty-four hours a day, or two evenings a week, or a few hours every weekend. It's staffed by counselors with years of experience, or high school students with a few training sessions and a great desire to help other kids in trouble. It's an outpatient center—a place where people can go for help with drug problems while still living at home.

*Outpatient programs* vary greatly. Some concentrate on providing information about cocaine and other drugs. Others hold group therapy sessions similar to those in TCs. A few provide individual counseling by doctors or psychologists who specialize in drug problems. Some teach techniques to handle stress, such as meditation and hypnosis. At one center, cocaholics rehearse ways to give up the drug. They pass a tray filled with little lines of white powder that looks exactly like cocaine. As they hand the tray around the circle, each person practices saying "No, thank you!" In another program, false cocaine that looks, smells, and tastes like the drug is given to addicts. Since the false cocaine has no effect, the doctors hope that the patients will no longer expect to get high when they see the real drug.

Surprisingly, one outpatient organization that many cocaine addicts go to for help is Alcoholics Anonymous. Alcoholics Anonymous, or AA, was founded in 1935 by an alcoholic who wanted to stay away from drinking "one day at a time." In the past fifty years, AA has helped many people stay sober. More recently, people who are addicted to cocaine and other drugs have gone to AA for help. Husbands and wives of cocaholics have also turned to Al-Anon, an organization for families of drug abusers, and Alateen, a group for children whose parents have drug problems. All AA, Al-Anon, and Alateen meetings are free, and strictly private. Members may attend as often as they wish. They may talk about their own or their family members' drug problems, or they may simply listen to others. The group provides support and guidance for all its members. A new organization, Cocaine Anonymous, follows the pattern of Alcoholics Anonymous but specializes in cocaine.

## COCAINE BLACKMAIL

An unusual treatment for cocaine addiction is being tested at the University of Colorado School of Medicine. Drug abusers who want to kick the habit write letters about their drug problems. They include the worst information they can think of. A doctor, for example, might describe a treatment he or she performed while high on coke. A lawyer might explain how a case was mishandled, and a police officer might tell about taking drugs on duty. Names, dates, and other facts are included. Then the letter is addressed to the person who might use the information. The doctor's letter would bear the address of the board that grants licenses to practice medicine. The lawyer's letter would be addressed to the Bar Association, and the police officer's to the chief of police. Other letters are addressed to relatives, employers, and even newspapers. The cocaine addict gives the letter to the doctor, with the understanding that the letter will not be mailed unless he or she uses the drug again. The doctor calls the patient in from time to time for a urine test; if any trace of cocaine is found, or if the patient fails to show up for the urine test, the letter is mailed. This ''blackmail'' method seems to be fairly successful. Knowing that they could lose their careers or whatever else is most dear to them, 80 percent of the patients stay off cocaine.

Other centers use a slightly different form of blackmail. The patient writes a check for a large amount of money to an organization that he or she dislikes. A Democrat might make a check for a Republican candidate; a pro-abortion activist might fill in the name of an anti-abortion group. Again, if the patient's urine test shows cocaine use, the check is mailed.

## IF YOU NEED HELP . . .

If you are having a problem with cocaine (or any other drug), don't be afraid to ask for help. Go to someone you can trust: your parents, school guidance counselor, church worker, or friend. If you afraid to tell someone you know that you have taken an illegal drug, contact one of the organizations on pages 60–62. Any information you give these groups will be kept strictly private.

## IF YOUR FRIEND NEEDS HELP . . .

If you know someone who is in trouble with cocaine, urge your friend to talk to an adult about the situation. (If your friend is an adult, suggest that he or she seek counseling from a doctor, church worker, or other expert.) Provide information from this book and from others like it so that the drug user will understand exactly what cocaine does to the body and the mind. Try to plan healthy activities that can replace the attraction of cocaine for your friend: suggest sports events, movies, and parties where people are not likely to use drugs. Above all, don't help your friend continue the drug habit. Don't lend money. Don't tell lies to cover up occasions when your friend has taken drugs. Don't allow your friend to take drugs when he or she is with you. If your friend refuses and takes cocaine anyway, walk away. This may seem cruel, but it is crueler still to stand by and watch people you love hurt themselves with cocaine.

# WHERE TO GET HELP

Organizations that help people with drug problems can be found in your local phone book under "Drug Abuse," "Cocaine," and "Drug Treatment Programs." If your phone book has a special section for city and state government phone numbers, check the same headings there. Here are some other addresses and phone numbers that may be helpful:

COCAINE HOTLINE
1-800-COCAINE
This is a toll-free number which may be called twenty-four hours a day for information and help with coke problems.

COKANON
1-212-265-2666
This recently formed organization is modelled on Alcoholics Anonymous. For information on local chapters, call the above number.

PHOENIX HOUSE
164 West 74th Street
New York, New York 10023
1-212-595-5810
Phoenix House is a therapeutic community for abusers of all types of drugs.

NATIONAL CLEARINGHOUSE FOR
DRUG ABUSE INFORMATION
P.O. Box 416
Kensington, Maryland 20795
1-301-443-6500
You can write or call the National Clearinghouse for free information on cocaine and other drugs.

ALCOHOLICS ANONYMOUS
P.O. Box 459
Grand Central Station
New York, New York 10017
Although AA was founded by and for alcoholics, many of its chapters now help cocaine abusers as well. Al-Anon and Ala-teen help the families of drug abusers. For information on a chapter near you, check the local phone book or write to the above address.

NATIONAL SELF-HELP CLEARINGHOUSE
33 West 42nd Street
Room 1206 - A
New York, New York 10036
1-212-840-1259
The Self-Help Clearinghouse will provide information on out-patient or residential programs for cocaine abusers.

HALE HOUSE CENTER
68 Edgecombe Avenue
New York, New York 10031
1-800-235-4433
Hale House is a center in Harlem, New York, that takes care of the children of drug addicts. Children whose parents or friends have problems with drugs can call the toll-free number above for expert help—between 9 A.M. and 9 P.M. Monday through Friday, and from 9 A.M. to 5 P.M. on Saturdays.

DAYTOP VILLAGE INC.
280 Broadway
Staten Island, New York
1-718-981-3136
Daytop operates many drug-abuse treatment programs.

COCAINE CENTER
152 Lombard
San Francisco, California
1-415-392-1658
Information and help with cocaine problems.

# GLOSSARY

*Addiction:* uncontrolled use of a drug in spite of dangerous consequences.

*Amphetamine:* a stimulant drug.

*Artificial respiration:* a first-aid technique in which air is forced into and out of the lungs of a person who has stopped breathing.

*Caffeine:* a drug found in coffee, tea, and some soft drinks that stimulates, or speeds up, the nervous system.

*Coca:* the name given to the plant or leaves from which cocaine is made.

*Cocaholic:* a cocaine addict.

*Cocaine:* a stimulant drug produced from the coca plant.

*Coke bugs:* sensation that tiny animals are crawling within or on the skin; a common hallucination among heavy users of cocaine.

*Crash:* a period of irritation, tiredness, and depression that follows a cocaine high.

*Dependency:* strong psychological need for a drug.

*Dopamine:* a brain chemical.

*Endorphins:* a natural pain reliever produced by the brain.

*Epinephrine:* a brain chemical.

*Erythroxylon coca:* scientific name of one variety of coca bush from which cocaine is made.

*Erythroxylon novogranatense:* scientific name of another variety of coca bush from which cocaine is made.

*Freebasing:* heating cocaine with other chemicals to release the cocaine base.

*Garbage head:* a person who takes more than one type of drug.

*Hallucination:* seeing, hearing, or sensing something that is not really there.

*Heroin:* a narcotic drug.

*Laundering:* moving money through several banks or businesses so that it cannot be traced.

*Lidocaine:* a local anesthetic.

*Local anesthetic:* a drug that numbs the area it touches without producing sleep.

*Mouth-to-mouth resuscitation:* a first-aid technique in which air is forced into and out of the lungs of a person who has stopped breathing.

*Mule:* someone who transports coca leaves to a laboratory for processing.

*Narcotic:* a drug that relieves pain and depresses or slows the nervous system.

*Norepinephrine:* a brain chemical.

*Novocaine:* a local anesthetic.

*Outpatient program:* drug treatment for people who continue to live at home.

*Procaine:* a local anesthetic.

*Residential drug treatment:* a "live-in" drug treatment program.

*Safe house:* house or apartment rented by smugglers as a warehouse for drugs.

*Seizure:* a period of unconsciousness in which the body shakes or becomes rigid.

*Sinus:* a hollow area near the nose and eye sockets.

*Snorting:* inhaling or breathing in cocaine through the nose.

*Speedball:* a mixture of cocaine and heroin.

*Stimulant:* a drug that excites the nervous system.

*Synapse:* the space between nerve cells in the brain.

*Therapeutic community:* a group of drug addicts who live together and try to break their drug habits.

*Tolerance:* the need for stronger and stronger doses of a drug to produce the same effect.

*Withdrawal symptom:* unpleasant sensation that occurs when use of an accustomed drug is discontinued.

# INDEX